The Story of a Special Day
Volume 318

November 13

*The 317ᵗʰ day of the year (318ᵗʰ in leap years).
There are 48 days remaining until the end of the year.*

by Michael Dobson

Timespinner
Press

Watch for e-book editions for Kindle, e-pub devices, and other formats from your favorite online booksellers.

For more information about the series, about us, or about your special day, please email us at editor@timespinnerpress.com.

Look for other volumes in *The Story of a Special Day*, coming often. See www.timespinnerpress.com for details and for the most recent information.

Table of Contents

For the definition of "O.S.," "CE," and "BCE" used with some dates , see the section "On Names and Dates."

Cover: A veteran salutes at the Vietnam Veterans Memorial in Washington DC. (Photo: Richard M. Everington, CC BY-SA 4.0) The Memorial was dedicated November 13, 1982 — the COVER STORY.

Quote of the Day

"There is no duty we so much underrate as
the duty of being happy."

Robert Louis Stevenson, novelist
born November 13, 1850

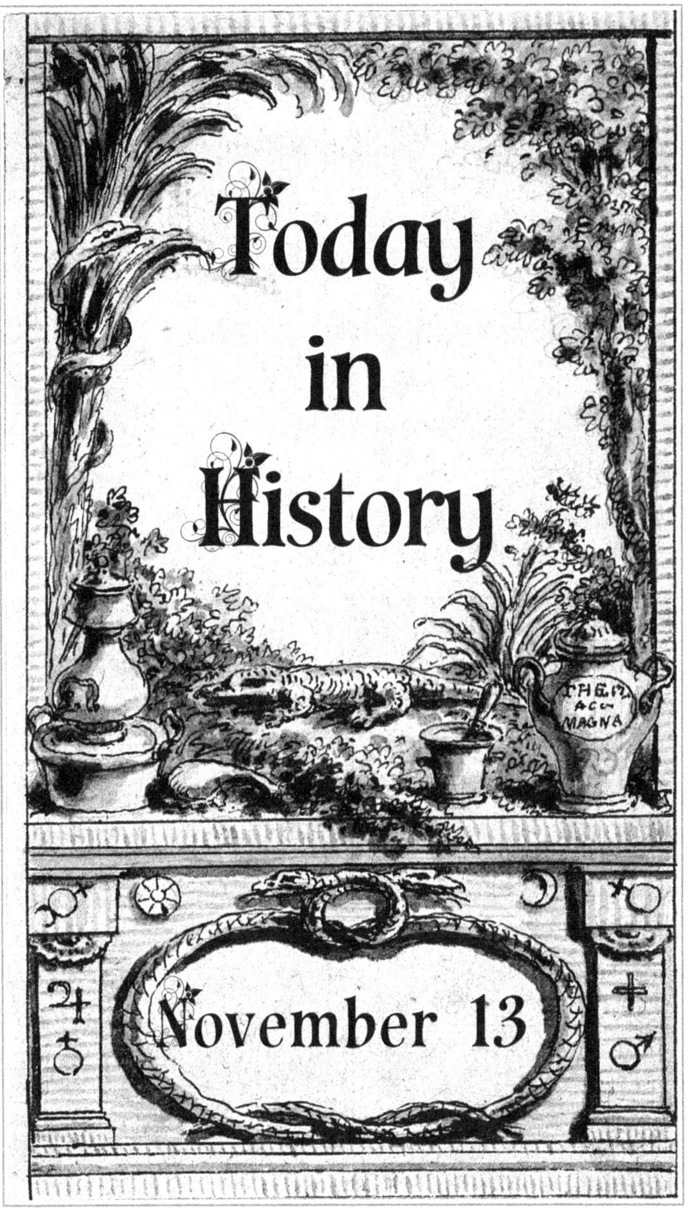
Today
in
History
November 13

Labors of the Months: November, by Simon Bening

November 13 in History

While some days of the year are more famous than others, every day of the year is filled with important, exciting, and unusual events, from religious awakenings to natural disasters, from wars to breakthroughs in technology, and from tragedy to triumph.

In this section, you'll learn about all the events that make November 13 important, including the special event that makes up our cover story or event of the day. Some events you may already know about, others may be new to you, but all of them are important parts of the history of the work.

Let's explore some of the reasons why November 13 is a very special day!

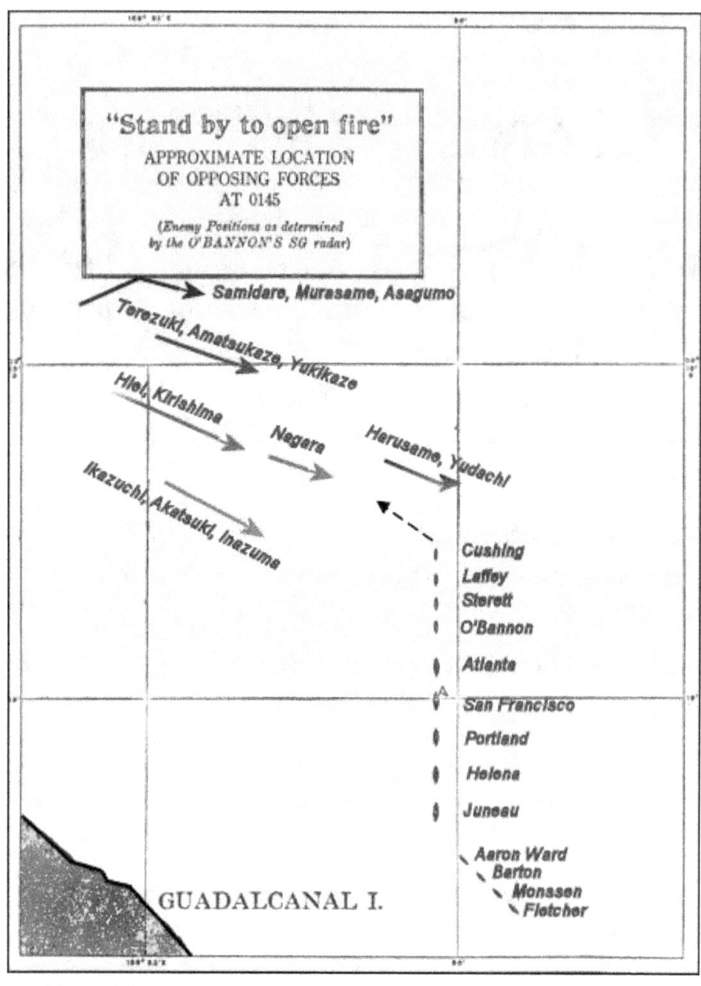

Map of the opening of the First Naval Battle of Guadalcanal,
November 13, 1942 (CC BY-SA 3.0)

What Happened on November 13?

From the creation of great works of engineering and art, to devastating wars and natural disasters, thousands of years of history have left their mark on each and every day. Here are some important events that occurred on November 13. (Items with a photo or illustration are boxed.)

1927 — New York's **Holland Tunnel**, a National Historic Civil and Mechanical Engineering Landmark,opened. Nearly 95,000 automobiles a day use the tunnel to cross the Hudson River between New Jersey and New York City. *(Photo next page.)*

1940 — Walt Disney's groundbreaking animation film *Fantasia* opens. Although initially unprofitable, its multiple releases over the years have made it the 22nd highest grossing film of all time, and the American Film Institute rates it among the top 100 greatest American films.

1942 — The **First Naval Battle of Guadalcanal**, sometimes known as the Battle of Friday the 13th, or 第三次ソロモン海戦 (*Dai-san-ji Soromon Kaisen*) in Japanese, was the decisive engagement in a series of naval battles between American and Japanese forces, pitting American Admiral William Halsey, Jr., against Japanese Admiral Isoroku Yamamoto. It prevented Japan from reinforcing forces on Guadalcanal Island.

1954 — The **first Rugby League World Cup** game is played in Paris. Great Britain defeated France by 16-12.

1956 — The US Supreme Court upholds the district court ruling in Browder v. Gayle, which declared Alabama racial segregation laws for buses were unconstitutional, which led to the **end of the Montgomery Bus Boycott**. *(Photo page 13.)*

1974 — Ronald DeFeo, Jr., murders his entire family in the town of Amityville, Long Island. The case was the basis for the book and film franchise *The Amityville Horror.*

A dog in the Holland Tunnel (Photo: H.L.I.T. CC BY-SA 2.0). The Holland Tunnel opened November 13, 1927

Event of the Day
1982 - Vietnam Memorial Dedicated

Veterans point out a familiar name
at the Vietnam Veterans Memorial

In 1979, four years after the end of the Vietnam War, a wounded Vietnam veteran named Jan Scruggs, inspired by the film The Deer Hunter, established the Vietnam Veterans Memorial Fund, Inc., to establish a memorial to the veterans of that war, and raised $8.4 million. By Act of Congress in 1980, three acres near the Lincoln Memorial were set aside for the proposed monument, and the US National Park Service established a design competition with a prize of $50,000.

There were four criteria: the memorial was to be reflective and contemplative in character, harmonize with its surroundings, contain the names of those who had died in the conflict or who were still missing, and make no political statement about the war.

Over 1,400 proposed designs were rated by a jury of eight architects and sculptors. Each design was identified only by number, and each juror independently rated each submission. The winning design — chosen unanimously — was by Maya Ying Lin, a 21-year old Yale University architecture student from Ohio. Lin proposed a memorial consisting of two long walls sunk into the earth, with the names of every US serviceperson killed in action or classified as missing.

The design, like the war it commemorated, was immediately controversial. A Vietnam veteran named Thomas Carhart referred to the proposed memorial as a "black gash of shame and sorrow." Former US Navy Secretary Jim Webb said, "I never in my wildest dreams imagined such a nihilistic slab of stone." Public outcry against the design led to the Secretary of the Interior, James Watt, refusing to issue a building permit for the project. The design was variously compared to a ditch or a gravestone, and the "V" shape of the memorial accused of being a subliminal anti-war peace sign. Maya Lin was called a "gook" and the jurors accused of being Communists.

Not all veterans felt that way. Many felt that the stark design was a solemn, dignified tribute to those who had fallen in the war. To resolve the controversy, the National Capital Planning Commission decided to add a statue and an American flag nearby.

The bronze statue, known as The Three Soldiers, was by Frederick Hart.

The Three Soldiers statue by Frederick Hart

Ground was broken March 26, 1982, and the memorial was dedicated on November 13, 1982. On opening day, thousands of Vietnam War veterans marched to the site. In spite of the controversy, public opinion shifted radically and the Vietnam Veterans Memorial quickly became one of the most visited memorials in the nation's capital. One veteran declared the memorial "the parade we never got."

The Memorial Wall originally contained 58,191 names. As additional information has been collected, more names have been added. As of May 2011, there were 58,272 names, of which about 1,200 are classified as missing. The Three Soldiers statue was unveiled on Veterans Day 1984. A third memorial was added in 1993: the Vietnam Women's Memorial, designed by Glenna Goodacre. An additional memorial plaque was added in 2004 to honor veterans who died after the war as a direct result of injuries suffered in Vietnam.

Visitors began leaving items at the memorial as soon as it opened, and several thousand items are left there each year. The National Park Service collects, catalogs, and stores all nonperishable items. Some of the items left there include a Harley-Davidson motorcycle with license plate HERO, a full-size replica "tiger cage" of the type used to imprison American POWs in North Vietnam, and even a Medal of Honor. Some of these items were put on display in a Smithsonian exhibition that ran from 1992 to 2003. Five traveling replicas of the Wall have been created; they visit hundreds of small towns and cities nationwide each year. Fixed replicas are located in New Jersey and Kansas, and a memorial of similar design to honor soldiers who fell in Iraq and Afghanistan is located in Irvine, California.

The Vietnam Veterans Memorial is ranked tenth on the "List of America's Favorite Architecture" by the American Institute of Architects.

1994 — Sweden votes to join the **European Union**.

2015 — A series of coordinated **terrorist attacks in Paris** kills 130 and wounds 368, not including the attackers. The Islamic State of Iraq and the Levant (ISIL or ISIS) claimed responsibility for the attacks.

MONTGOMERY BUS BOYCOTT — US President Barack Obama sits in the Rosa Parks bus. (Photo: Pete Souza)

Quote of the Day

"Since love grows within you, so beauty grows. For love is the beauty of the soul."

Saint Augustine, theologian and philosopher
born November 13, 354

Births
and
Deaths
AC· 12
ACCA
MAGNA
November 13

Saint Augustine by Baltasar del Águila. Saint Augustine was born
November 13, 354 — the PERSON OF THE DAY

Notable November 13 People

With the current world population at about seven billion people, on average about 19 million people also celebrate their birthdays on November 13 — and that isn't counting millions and millions who came before! No matter when you were born, you share your birthday with many special people whose accomplishments (and occasionally embarrassments) have been noted as part of history.

In this section, you'll meet fascinating people who share your birthday, or who died on this day in history. They're organized by what they're famous for, and then in reverse chronological order from most recent to earliest. Those who are shown in photographs or artwork have a box around them. We don't have photos of everyone, so please forgive us if your favorite person is missing.

Some of these people you've heard of, others will be new to you, but they all make up an important part of the reason that November 13 is a truly special day!

Robert Louis Stevenson, writer, born November 13, 1850

Who Was Born on November 13?

Government and Law

Iskander Mirza, first President of Pakistan, also first Indian to graduate Sandhurst Military Academy, first Indian to command British troops, and first Indian to join the Indian Political Service. Oversaw military efforts in the first Pakistan-India war in 1947. Deposed in 1958 in a coup. *(1899*)*

Iskander Mirza

---

* Iskander Mirza died on his 70th birthday, November 13, 1969. His story is told in the book *From Plassey to Pakistan*, by his son Humayun Mirza, published by Timespinner Press. See "Other Books by Timespinner Press" for details.

Louis Brandeis, known as the "People's Lawyer," associate justice of the US Supreme Court, known for helping to develop the legal concept of the "right to privacy." *(1856)*

Maharaja Ranjit Singh, known as the "Lion of Punjab," founded and built the Sikh Empire in the Indian subcontinent. *(1780)*

Maharaja Ranjit Singh

Edward III, king of England from 1327 to 1377, built England into a major military power and started the Hundred Years' War. *(1312)*

Literature and Journalism

Peter Arnett, journalist who received a Pulitzer Prize in International Reporting for his coverage of the Vietnam War. *(1934)*

Pat Reid, British Army officer during World War II who wrote about his experiences as a POW who escaped from Colditz Castle in two best-selling books, which were later the basis of a film and TV series. *(1910)*

William Bradford Huie, Alabama journalist and novelist known *The Americanization of Emily, The Revolt of Mamie Stover,* and *The Execution of Private Slovik,* all of which were made into films. *(1910)*

Robert Louis Stevenson, Scottish novelist, poet, and travel writer whose best known works include *Treasure Island* and *The Strange Case of Dr. Jekyll and Mr. Hyde.* (1850) *(Photo page 18.)*

Military and Adventure

Jesús García Corona, Mexican railroad brakeman who died while preventing a train loaded with dynamite from exploding, revered as a national hero in Mexico. *(1881)*

Joseph Hooker, Union general during the American Civil War, best remembered for his defeat by Confederate General Robert E. Lee at the Battle of Chancellorsville. *(1814)*

Performing Arts

Jimmy Kimmel, comedian and host of the talk show *Jimmy Kimmel Live! (1967)*

Whoopi Goldberg, actress and comedian nominated for 13 Emmy awards, and one of the few ever to win an Emmy, a Grammy, an Oscar, and a Tony. Her best known roles include the film *The Color Purple* and *Sister Act,* as well as host of the talk show *The View. (1955)*

Whoopi Goldberg (Photo: David Shankbone CC BY-SA 3.0)

Chris Noth, actor known for his roles on *Sex and the City* and *The Good Wife. (1954)*

Art Malik, Pakistani-British actor best known for his role as Hari Kumar in *The Jewel in the Crown. (1952)*

Joe Mantegna, stage and screen actor known for roles in *The Godfather Part III,* the television series *Criminal Minds,* and *The Last Don. (1947)*

Dack Rambo, actor known for television work including *All My Children, Another World,* and *Dallas. (1941)*

Jean Seberg, actress who starred in 34 films in America and Europe; targeted in the FBI COINTELPRO project as retaliation for her support of the Black Panther Party. *(1938)*

Jean Seberg

Garry Marshall, best known as a producer of television shows including *Happy Days* and *The Odd Couple*, and as director of such films as *Pretty Woman, Runaway Bride,* and the *Princess Diaries. (1934)*

Richard Mulligan, actor known for his roles in the sitcoms *Soap* and *Empty Nest. (1932)*

Linda Christian, actress known as the first Bond girl, appearing in the 1954 television adaptation of *Casino Royale. (1923)*

Oskar Werner, Austrian actor best known for his roles in such films as *The Spy Who Came in from the Cold* and *Fahrenheit 451. (1922)*

Jack Elam, American actor best known for his many roles as a villain in Western films, including *Once Upon a Time in the West* and *High Noon. (1920)*

Jack Elam in *Kansas City Confidential*

Amelia Bence, Argentine film actress considered one of the great divas of the Golden Age of Argentine Cinema *(1914)*

Hermione Badderley, British character actress whose notable films include *Room at the Top* (for which she received an Academy Award nomination as Best Supporting Actress) and as a maid in *Mary Poppins*. *(1906)*

Gertrude Olmstead, American silent film actress who appeared in 56 films, most famously opposite Rudolph Valentino in the 1925 film *Cobra*. *(1897)*

Gertrude Olmstead, by George Grantham Bain

Edwin Booth, older brother of Lincoln assassin John Wilkes Booth, considered one of the greatest American actors as well as the greatest Hamlet of the 19th century. *(1833)*

Edwin Booth

Religion and Philosophy

Fred Phelps, founded the Westboro Baptist Church, best known for anti-gay activism, including deliberate disruptions of funerals, and for its signature slogan, "God Hates Fags."*(1929)*

Person of the Day
Augustine of Hippo (354)

One of the most important early Church Fathers in western Christianity, Saint Austine was a highly influential writer, theologian, and philosopher. He is recognized as a saint by the Roman Catholic Church, the eastern Orthodox Church, and the Anglican Communion.

Augustine was a Berber, born in North Africa under Roman rule. His mother was a Christian; his father was a pagan who converted on his deathbed. He led a hedonistic lifestyle in his youth (during which he made his famous prayer, "Grant me chastity and continence, but not yet"), and dabbled in various heresies, including Manechaeism. He had a son with a long-time lover, but subsequently decided to become a celibate priest.

Augustine was known for his brilliance almost from the beginning. After completing his education, he taught in Carthage and Rome before joining the imperial court at Milan as a professor of rhetoric.

When he was 31, he converted to Christianity, and wrote his first major work, *Confessions*, an account of his conversion and an important milestone in the development of autobiography. He returned to North Africa as a priest and later bishop of Hippo Regius, in present-day Algeria, where he remained until his death in 430.

In addition to an active role in the life of the church, Augustine became one of the most prolific scholars of the early church. His works covered theological anthropology, original sin, ecclesiology, predestination, and other topics. Besides his *Confessions,* he is best known for his 22-volume work *The City of God* and for *On the Trinity.* He was a major influence on later theologians and philosophers including Thomas Aquinas, Bertrand Russell, and Martin Heidegger.

Aquinas was canonized (made a saint) in 1298, and has also been proclaimed as a Doctor of the Church and Church Father. He is the patron saint of brewers, printers, and theologians. His feast day is August 28 in the western church, June 15 in the eastern church, and November 4 in the Assyrian church.

Saint Augustine, by Justus van Gent

Science and Technology

Edward Aldelbert Doisy, American biochemist who shared the 1943 Nobel Prize in Physiology or Medicine for his co-discovery of vitamin K. *(1856)*

Sports

Vinny Testaverde, Heisman Trophy winning quarterback who played 21 seasons in the NFL. *(1963)*

Jay Sigel, golfer known for his long career in amateur golf before turning pro at the age of 50 *(1943)*

Buck O'Neil, first baseman and manager in the Negro American League, later the first African-American coach in major league baseball. His life was documented in the award-winning 2007 book *The Soul of Baseball. (1911)*

Buck O'Neil

Self-Portrait, Camille Pissaro

Who Died on November 13?

Art and Letters

Margaret Wise Brown, children's book author best known for her picture books with Clement Hurd, *Goodnight Moon* and *The Runaway Bunny.* *(1952)*

Camille Pissaro, Danish-French impressionist and neo-impressionist painter known both for his own work and for his leadership and support of other important figure in the Impressionist movement. *(1903)*

Government and Military

Iskander Mirza, first president of Pakistan, born and died on the same day of the year. *(Photo and additional information on page 19) (1969)*

Daniel J. Callaghan, US Navy admiral and former navy aide to President Franklin D. Roosevelt; received the Medal of Honor for his actions during the Naval Battle of Guadalcanal *(see page 7). (1942)*

Prince Henry the Navigator, Portuguese nobleman whose oversight of Portugal's exploration and maritime trade made him the main initiator of the Age of Discoveries. *(1460)*

Malcolm III of Scotland, King of Scots for 35 years, and the historical character associated with the character of Malcolm in Shakespeare's *Macbeth.* *(1093)*

History and Anthropology

Vine Deloria Jr., Native American theologian and historian known for his 1969 book *Custer Died for Your Sins: An Indian Manifesto,* which brought Native American issues to national prominence. *(2005)*

Margaret Murray, Egyptologist and anthropologist dubbed "the Grand Old Woman of Egyptology" and the "Grandmother of Wicca" for her research into pre-Christian pagan religions. *(1963)*

Bernard DeVoto, historian and author noted for his books about the American West. *(1955)*

Music

Leon Russell, rock musician and songwriter inducted into both the Rock and Roll Hall of Fame and the Songwriters Hll of Fame for his highly successful 60-year career. *(2016)*

Ol' Dirty Bastard, rapper and music producer who helped found the rap group Wu-Tang Clan. He took his professional name from the title of the 1980 martial arts film *Ol' Dirty and the Bastard.* *(1998)*

Leon Russell

Performing Arts

Valerie Hobson, English actress best known for roles in films ranging from *Bride of Frankenstein* to *Kind Hearts and Coronets.* Her second husband, British member of parliament John Profumo, was at the center of highly publicized sex scandal, leading to their retreat from public life. *(1998)*

Vittorio De Sica, Italian director and actor, best known for his 1948 film *The Bicycle Thief*, cited as one of the most influential films in cinema history. He was nominated for a Best Supporting Actor Oscar for his role as Major Rinaldi in 1957's *A Farewell to Arms*. *(1974)*

Lila Lee, leading lady during the silent film and early sound film eras, nicknamed "Cuddles." Best known for her 1922 role in *Blood and Sand*, opposite Rudolph Valentino. *(1963)*

Lila Lee

Science and Industry

Karen Silkwood, chemical technician and labor activist in the nuclear industry who raised concerns about worker health and safety. Her mysterious death led to a highly publicized lawsuit, as well a Oscar-nominated 1983 film *Silkwood,* in which she was portrayed by Meryl Streep. *(1963)*

Sports

Alvin Dark, baseball shortstop and manager known as "the Swamp Fox." Played fourteen seasons for five NL teams from 1946 through 1960. named Rookie of the Year in 1948. *(2014)*

Bowman Gum card, 1953

Red Holzman, head coach of the New York Knicks from 1967 to 1982, leading the team to two NBA championships. Named one of the top ten coaches in NBA history, and was inducted into the Basketball Hall of Fame. *(1998)*

Quote of the Day

"If we would guide by the light of
reason, we must let our minds be bold."

Louis Brandeis, US Supreme Court justice
born November 13, 1856

Holidays
Around
the World
November 13
THE 12
ACC
MAGNA

Friday the Thirteenth (Photo: W. J. Pilsak, CC BY-SA 3.0)

Holidays Around the World

If you're looking for a reason to take your special day off, you should know that every single day is a holiday somewhere in the world! Here's some of what you can celebrate on November 13!

Friday the Thirteenth

While November 13 doesn't come on Friday every year, sooner or later, every 13th day of the month eventually lands on the dreaded last day of the week.

Friday the 13th is considered an unlucky day in many (but not all) Western nations. Both the number 13 and Friday have a history of being thought unlucky, so when you put the two togethe.... The idea that Friday is unlucky seems to be a maritime superstition — sailors believed it was unlucky to start a voyage on a Friday.

As far as the number 13 goes, there are a number of theories.One theory is that it refers to the 13 people around the table at the Last Supper, one of whom (Judas) would shortly betray Jesus. Others point out that on Friday, October 13, 1307, the Knights Templar were arrested, and many of them were later tortured and killed.

Fear of the number thirteen is common enough that a psychological condition, *triskaidekaphobia*, is named for it! (Fear of Friday the 13th in particular is known as *paraskevidekatriaphobia*.) According to some researchers, between 17 and 21 million people in the US alone are bothered by Friday the 13th. Fear of thirteen is so common that many tall buildings skip 13 when numbering floors.

In Spanish-speaking countries, as well as in Greece, they worry about Tuesday the 13th (*martes trece*) instead — though either way, June 13 qualifies. In Italy, though, 13 is a lucky number — but watch out for Friday the 17th!

November 13 General Events

Sadie Hawkins Day

Some sources list November 13 as Sadie Hawkins Day, but others list November 15. Either way, Sadie Hawkins Day originated in Al Capp's comic strip Li'l Abner. On Sadie Hawkins day, single women chased bachelor men. If a woman caught a man and dragged him over the finish line before sundown, he had to marry her.

In real life, Sadie Hawkins Day, and associated events like Sadie Hawkins dances, involves a switch of traditional gender roles, in which women ask men to be their dates. The first known Sadie Hawkins event took place in 1938, only a year after the first Sadie Hawkins Day appeared in the comic.

Sadie Hawkins Day from Al Capp's Li'l Abner. (Copyright © United Features Syndicate)

World Kindness Day

November 13 is World Kindness Day in many
nations. Sponsored by the World Kindness
Movement, it has been observed since 1998.

November 13 Food Holidays

National Indian Pudding Day (US)

In the United States, almost every day of the year is
dedicated to a particular food. (Some other countries
do this also, but not every day.) Sponsored by
manufacturers, retailers, farmers, or simply fans,
these days are often proclaimed by the President,
Congress, state governors, or mayors. Given that
there are more different foods than days of the year,
some days honor more than one kind of food!

Indian pudding is made of cornmeal and
molasses, baked, and often mixed with fruit like
apples or raising. It is baked

The name of Indian pudding doesn't actually
refer to Native Americans. Instead, it's a reference to
the principle ingredient. Cornmeal used to be called
Indian meal, because corn originated in the New
World.

Honorary Food Months

In addition, the entire month of November is used to
celebrate numerous foods. Here's a list of what to eat
in the month of November!

- National Georgia Pecan Month
- National Peanut Butter Lover's Month

- National Pepper Month
- National Pomegranate Month
- National Raisin Bread Month
- Sweet Potato Awareness Month
- Vegan Month

- National Fun With Fondue Month

Cheese Fondue (for NATIONAL FUN WITH FONDUE MONTH).
(CC BY-SA 2.0)

Religious Feast Days and Holidays

Feroniae (ancient Rome)

The Roman goddess Feronia was associated with wildlife, fertility, health, and abundance. She granted freedom to slaves and civil rights to the most humble. Her festival was held on the ides of November (November 13) during the Plebean Games.

Saint Days

Each day in the year is considered a feast day for one or more saints. November 13 is the feast day of Saints Brice of Tours, Frances Xavier Cabrini, Homobonus, Quintian of Rodez, John Chrysostom (Eastern Orthodox), Stanislaus Kostka, Charles Simeon (Church of England), and the Hundred Thousand Martyrs of Tblisi (Georgian Orthodox).

Moveable and Multi-Day Events

Some events take place over a specific week or time period. Start and finish dates may vary from year to year. Some events occur on different days each year (such as "fourth Saturday of a month"). These events sometimes include or take place on November 13.

Week-Long Celebrations

- Customer Service Week (US and Kenya)
- Geography Awareness Week
- National Nurse Practitioners Week
- National Split Pea Soup Week
- Mental Illness Awareness Week (US)

November Honorary Months

Presidents, Congresses, and nations around the world issue proclamations recognizing particular months to honor certain causes. These events generally fall in October, though honorary months do come and go. Holidays established by states and nonprofit organizations are listed if verified.

If not otherwise specified, all months are US. There is some variation from year to year; some celebratory months get added and others get dropped. Two places to get up to date information are the current edition of *Chase's Calendar of Events* or the website Brownielocks.

Here are some honorary designations for November.

- Adopt a Turkey Month
- Aviation History Month
- Epilepsy Awareness Month
- Historic Bridge Awareness Month
- Military Family Appreciation Month
- National Adoption Month
- National Diabetes Month
- National Family Literacy Month
- National Hospice Month
- National Memoir Writing Month
- National Novel Writing Month (NaNoWriMo)
- World Sponge Month

Movable Events

Volkstrauertag (Germany)

Germany's People's Day of Mourning is a public holiday observed two Sundays before the first day of Advent, so it can occur anywhere between November 13 to November 19. On this day, Germans commemorate members of the German armed forces and civilians who died in armed conflicts, including victims of violent oppression.

Other moveable events that sometimes fall on November 13 include:

- Domino Day (2nd Friday)

- International Day of Prayer for the Persecuted Church (2nd Sunday)
- National Young Readers Day (2nd Tuesday)
- World Orphans Day (2nd Monday)

Dominoes, for DOMINO DAY (Photo: Gaz, CC BY-SA 3.0)

Quote of the Day

"November's night is dark and drear,
The dullest month of all the year."

Letitia Elizabeth Landon,
in *Traits and Trials of Early Life* (1836)

47

November, from the *Brevarium Grimani* (c.1510)

November: The Eleventh Month

When shrieked
The bleak November winds, and smote the woods,
And the brown fields were herbless, and the shades
That met above the merry rivulet
Were spoiled, I sought, I loved them still; they seemed
Like old companions in adversity.

William Cullen Bryant, A Winter Piece

In Latin, *novem* means "nine," so it may seem strange that November is the eleventh month of the year. The original Roman calendar started in March, making November indeed the ninth month. No one is completely sure when the start of the year was moved to January, but the traditional name of November stuck.

In the northern hemisphere, November is a month in late autumn. In the southern hemisphere, November is in the springtime. May is its opposite month; spring in the north and fall in the south.

If it's not a Leap Year, November always starts on the same day of the week as February. If it is a leap year, November starts on the same day of the week as March.

November in Other Cultures

The month of November has different names in different languages. Some nations use calendars other than the Gregorian, and their months may overlap with November. In lunar-based calendars, such as the Islamic calendar, months move through the seasons. Still, many languages often have a word for November itself.

Arabic: نوفمبر (Nūfambar)

Chinese and Japanese: 十一月

Croatian: Studeni

Czech and Polish: Listopad

Finnish: Marraskuu

Greek: Νοέμβριος

Hebrew: נובמבר

Hindi: नवंबर

Old English: Blōtmōnaþ

Russian: ноябрь

November Sayings and Superstitions

Here are some sayings and superstitions associated with the month of November

- "A November bride will be liberal and kind, but sometimes cold."

- "Married in veils of November mist/Fortune your wedding ring has kissed."

- "If you wed in bleak November, only joys will come, remember."

November, by Eugène Grasset

November Symbols

Birthstone: Topaz (primarily yellow), and citrine (left). Topaz is associated with strength, tenacity, dedication and resilience. Citrine is supposed to encourage vitality and promote good health.

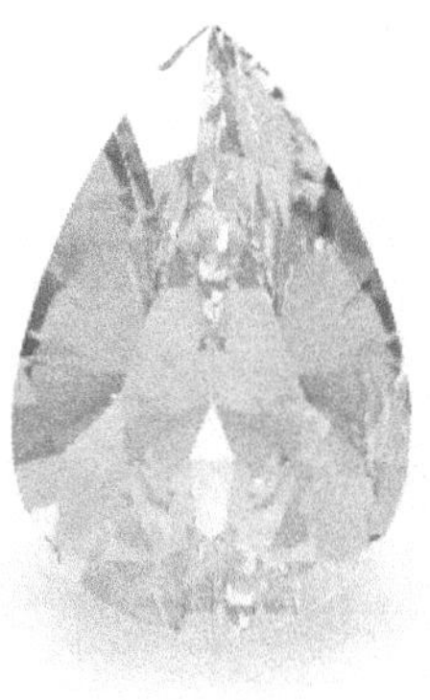

Citrine

Birth Flower: Chrysanthemum. The Chrysanthemum is associated with compassion, friendship,and joy. Red is for love, white for innocence, and yellow for unrequited love.

Chrysanthemums, by Claude Monet

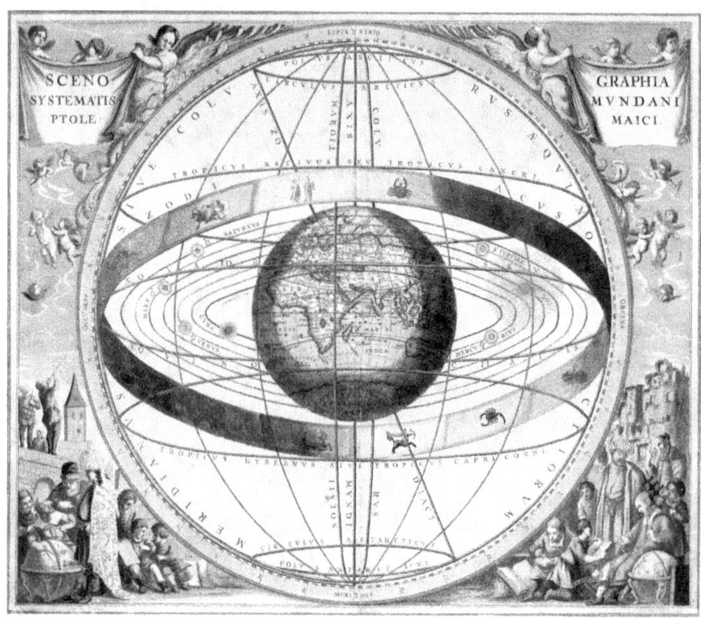

Scenography of the Ptolemaic Cosmography, by Johannes van Loon, based on Andreas Cellarius's *Harmonia Macrocosmica,* 1660

November 13 Zodiac Signs

From the perspective of someone on Earth, the Sun appears to move through the sky throughout the year, along a path astronomers call the *ecliptic plane*. The ecliptic plane is divided into twelve constellations, known as the zodiac, based on traditionally observed patterns of stars. On your birthday, you can't see your constellation, because it's in the daytime sky.

The zodiac was first developed by Babylonian astronomers about 2,500 years ago. Because they were unaware that the Earth wobbles like a spinning top (known as *precession*), they didn't make allowance for the fact that the Sun's path through the zodiac changes over time.

That means there are now two sets of dates for your birth sign. The *tropical dates* are the original Babylonian dates; the *sidereal dates* tell you where the Sun actually appears as it moves along its annual path.

For November 13, the tropical sign is **Scorpio** and the sidereal sign is **Libra**.

Libra

Tropical September 23 to October 23
Sidereal October 16 to November 15

The Babylonians considered Libra, the Scales, to be sacred to the sun god Shamash, patron of truth and justice. The Romans reassigned the scales to Astraea, the celestial virgin, better known as Virgo.

Libra is an air sign, and people born under this sign are supposed to be extroverts, socially graceful, and just. Librans are supposed to be compatible with the other air signs of Gemini and Aquarius.

Scorpio

Tropical October 23 to November 21
Sidereal November 16 to December 15

Scorpio, the Scorpion, appears in the Greek myth of the hunter Orion. Because Orion had touched the robes of the goddess Artemis, in revenge, the goddess had the scorpion kill Orion. As a reward, she placed the scorpion in the sky, where it chases Orion through the eternal night.

Scorpio is a fire sign, and people born under this sign are supposed to be determined, reserved, loyal, and secretive. Scorpios are supposed to be compatible with the water signs of Pisces and Capricorn.

Illustration by Edward Penfield

What Day of the Week is November 13?

On what day of the week does November 13 fall?

Surprisingly, this isn't an easy question. Because the calendar year is 365 days long (366 in leap years), it doesn't divide evenly by the seven days of the week.

Also, the Earth goes around the Sun in about 365-1/4 days, so a calendar tends to drift over time. That's why the same date falls on different weekdays in different years.

This is made even more complicated by a change in calendars that took place in 1582. Our modern calendar has its roots in ancient Rome, in a calendar reform conducted by Julius Caesar. Caesar commissioned mathematicians to attack the problem, and they came up with the idea of leap years, and thus standardized the calendar for centuries to come. This was called the Julian calendar.

Over time, however, the small errors in Caesar's calculation compounded. That's why Pope Gregory XIII commissioned the Gregorian calendar, used in most of the world today. Some countries converted in 1582, when the calendar was first developed; some converted later; other still haven't changed.

Gregorian and Julian aren't the only types of calendars. The Hebrew year, the Islamic year, and many other calendars are used in different parts of the world and among different people.

You can convert Gregorian dates to other calendars, including the Hebrew calendar, the Islamic calendar, and even the Mayan calendar by visiting the Fourmilab Calendar Converter at http://www.fourmilab.ch/documents/calendar/.

Chinese calendar systems are quite complex and have changed several times; a full discussion is far beyond the scope of this book. If you're interested, you can find information here: http://www.hermetic.ch/cal_stud/chinese_cal.htm.

On Names and Dates

Historians use "CE" (Common Era) and "BCE" (Before the Common Era) instead of the more common "AD" (Anno Domini, or Year of Our Lord) and "BC" (Before Christ), reflecting the fact that the year-numbering system established by the Gregorian calendar is used throughout the world in many countries not culturally Christian.

The CE/BCE designation dates back to at least 1708, and has been adopted as a standard by the United Nations and the Universal Postal Union. Because this series of books covers events and people of all nations and cultures, we use the CE/BCE terms.

The abbreviation "O.S." ("Old Style") on some dates refers to the fact that the Russian Empire did not switch from the Julian to the Gregorian calendar at the same time as the rest of Europe, and therefore some figures and events have two dates.

Also, in the Julian calendar in England in the 16th century, the year began on March 25 rather than January 1. To avoid confusion with Gregorian dates, dates between January and March were often written using both years.

People and events whose original names are not in the Western alphabet have their native names (where possible) in the appropriate script shown in parenthesis. If you are using an e-reader to access an electronic version of this book, all characters don't always display on all devices.

A 50-year brass perpetual calendar.

Quote of the Day

"Time is an illusion, lunchtime doubly so."

Douglas Adams,
from *The Hitchhiker's Guide to the Galaxy*

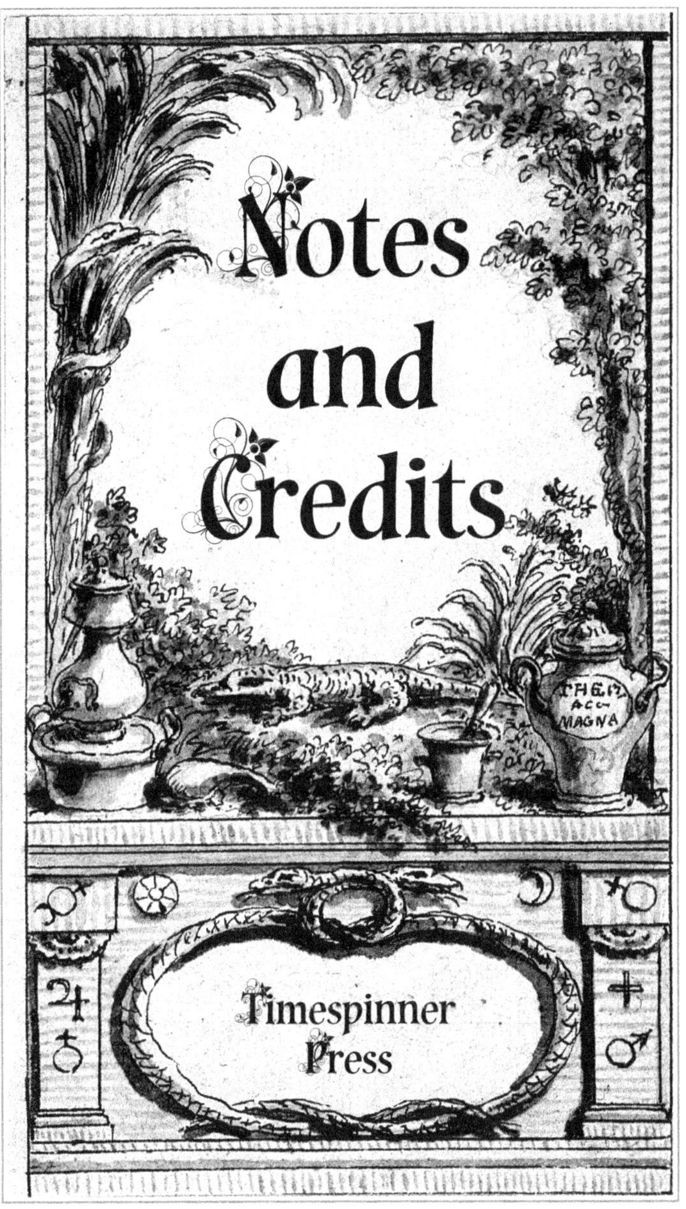

Notes
and
Credits
Timespinner
Press

Cartoon by John T. McCutcheon

Copyright, Credit, and Contact

Follow Us

Our blog "This Day in History" (http://timespinnerpress.com/this-day-in-history/) features short articles on events and people associated with each day, and updates several times each week. Also subscribe to the "Quote of the Day" at http://timespinnerpress.com/quote-of-the-day/. You can get daily links by following us on Facebook at TimespinnerPress, or on Twitter as @sidewisethinker.

Contact Us

Find an error or a format problem? Want information about the series, about us, or about when the volume for your special day might be available? Please email us at editor@timespinnerpress.com. (We also take requests if your special day isn't yet complete. Please give us at least six weeks' notice if possible.)

Sources

We owe a great debt to Wikipedia, which is our first stop for research. We attempt to make independent confirmation of all important dates and facts through a variety of other sources.

Other sources we frequently use include the Library of Congress; "on this day" listings from *Encyclopedia Britannica,* the *New York Times,* and the BBC; Omniglot for the names of months in other languages; *Chase's Calendar of Events;* and, of course, the always essential Google.

All art and photographs are either in the public domain, used under a Creative Commons license, or with a "fair use" justification, and most frequently come from Wikimedia Commons and the Library of Congress Prints and Photographs Division.

Attribution is provided where possible, or as requested by the copyright owner, or when there is particular historical significance, listed below. For information about any particular illustration or photograph, please contact us.

Credits

1. The cover photograph of a saluting veteran at the Vietnam Veterans Memorial was taken in 2016 by Richard M. Everington, and is used here under CC BY-SA 4.0.

2. The illustration of the month of November used on the back cover is from the French Gothic illuminated manuscript *Les Très Riches Heures du duc de Berry* by the Limbourg Brothers, Jean Colombe, and an intermediate painter whose name is lost to history. It is in the public domain because its copyright has expired.

3. The box graphic used on the first page is from a 1916 pamphlet entitled "Divorce versus Democracy" authored by G. K. Chesterton, originally published in London by the Society of St. Peter and St. Paul. It is in the public domain in the US because it was published prior to 1923, and is in the public domain in all countries (including the country of origin) in which the copyright time is the author's life plus 70 years or less.

4. The graphic design for the section pages in this book is from a design originally created for a pharmacy label. It is courtesy of Wellcome Images (ICV No 11073, photo V0010813), and is used here under CC BY-SA 4.0.

5. The painting "November" from *Labors of the Month* by Simon Bening, was originally published in the first half of the 16th century, and is in the public domain because its copyright has expired.

6. The map of the opening of the first Naval Battle of
    Guadalcanal is based on a US Navy map, modified by
    Wikimedia Commons users "Cla68" and "Pibwl." The
    underlying map is in the public domain as a work of the US
    government; the modifications are used here under the CC
    BY-SA 3.0 license.

7. The 2015 photograph of a dog in the Holland Tunnel was
    taken by "H. L. I. T." It is used here under CC BY-SA 2.0.

8. The photograph of US veterans at the Vietnam Veterans
    Memorial is in the public domain as an official photograph
    taken by the US Department of Defense. It carries the
    identification number 060911-D-7203T-030.

9. The photograph of the Three Soldiers statue by Frederick
    Hart is in the public domain as an official photograph taken
    by Sgt. Michael J. Cardin of the US Department of Defense.
    It carries the identification number 100708-D-7377C-007a.

10. The 2012 photograph of US President Barack Obama sitting
    in the Rosa Parks bus at the Henry Ford Museum was taken
    by White House photographer Pete Souza, and is in the
    public domain as a work created by an employee of the US
    government as part of that person's official duties.

11. The 1563 painting of Saint Augustine by Baltasar del Águila
    is in the public domain because its copyright has expired.
    The original is in the collection of the Cordoba Fine Arts
    Museum, Spain.

12. The 1885 photograph of Robert Louis Stevenson is in the
    public domain because its copyright has expired.

13. The 1956 photograph of Iskander Mirza is in the public
    domain because its copyright has expired, according to the
    Pakistan Copyright Ordinance, 1962, as amended by
    Copyright (Amendment) Ordinance, 2000.

14. The painting of Ranjit Singh is in the public domain because
    its copyright has expired. The artist is unknown.

15. The 2008 photograph of Whoopi Goldberg is by David
    Shankbone, and is used here under CC BY-SA 3.0.

16. The 1972 screenshot from *Camorra* is in the public domain in
    Italy, its country of origin, because its term of copyright has
    expired.

17. The 1952 trailer screenshot from *Kansas City Confidential* is in the public domain because it was first published in the US between 1923 and 1977 without a copyright notice. Traditionally, film trailers are not copyrighted because of the way they are intended to be used.

18. The 1927 photograph of Gertrude Olmstead by George Grantham Bain is in the public domain according the the Library of Congress. It is from the George Grantham Bain collection at the Library, with digital ID ggbain.25626.

19. The 1870 photograph of Edwin Booth as Hamlet is by J. Gurney & Son. It is in the public domain because its copyright has expired.

20. The painting of St. Augustine by Justus van Gent was painted circa 1474, and is in the public domain because its copyright has expired. The original is in the collection of the Louvre.

21. The photograph of Buck O'Neil is in the public domain because it was first published in the US between 1923 and 1977 without a copyright notice.

22. The 1873 self-portrait of Camille Pissarro is in the public domain because its copyright has expired. The original is in the Musée d'Orsay, Paris.

23. The 1973 publicity photograph of Leon Russell is in the public domain because it was first published in the US between 1923 and 1977 without a copyright notice. Traditionally, publicity photographs are not copyrighted because of the way they are intended to be used.

24. The cover of the February 1922 issue of *Photoplay* is in the public domain because its copyright has expired.

25. The 1953 Bowman baseball card of Alvin Dark is in the public domain because it was published in the US between 1923 and 1953, and although there may or may not have been a copyright notice, the copyright was not renewed.

26. The photograph of Friday the 13th circled in a calendar was taken by W. J. Pilsak, and is used here under CC BY-SA 3.0.

27. The panel from *Li's Abner* by Al Capp is copyright © by United Features Syndicate, and is used here under "fair use" provisions of US copyright law. No free alternative can exist because the characters are copyrighted and trademarked. It

is a low-resolution image not suitable for the creation of counterfeit merchandise or the creation of illegal copies, it does not limit the copyright owner's rights to sell the comic strip in any way, and it is a significant image of a historical event.

28. The 2009 photograph of cheese fondue is by "The Junes" and modified by "Zitronenpresse."It is used here under CC BY-SA 2.0.

29. The photograph of dominoes is by "Gaz," and is used here under CC BY-SA 3.0.

30. The painting "November" is from the *Brevarium Grimani*, circa 1510, and is in the public domain because its copyright has expired.

31. The 1896 postcard "November" by Eugène Grasset is in the public domain because its copyright has expired.

32. The photograph of a citrine is by Les Facettes and is used here under CC BY-SA 3.0.

33. The 1882 painting of chrysanthemums by Claude Monet is in the public domain because its copyright has expired. The painting is in the collection of the Metropolitan Museum of Art, New York.

34. The celestial sphere is from *Scenography of the Ptolemaic Cosmography,* by Johannes van Loon, based on Andreas Cellarius's *Harmonia Macrocosmica*, 1660. It is in the public domain because its copyright has expired.

35. The 1906 automobile calendar is by Edward Penfield, and is in the collection of the Library of Congress Prints and Photographs Division. It is in the public domain because its copyright has expired.

36. The 50-year perpetual calendar photograph is in the public domain.

37. The cartoon by John T. McCutcheon is from his 1905 collection *The Mysterious Stranger and Other Cartoons by John T. McCutcheon*. It is in the public domain because its copyright has expired.

License Description and Terms

Aside from material purely in the public domain, photographs and other material in this book are used under specific licenses permitting free use, usually with an attribution requirement. For full text and terms of these licenses, click or enter the appropriate links below. If you believe there is an error in the copyright status or attribution of any of these images, please email us.

- Creative Commons Attribution 2.0 Generic (CC-BY 2.0): http://creativecommons.org/licenses/by/2.0/deed.en
- Creative Commons Attribution-Share Alike 3.0 Generic (CC-BY-SA 3.0): http://creativecommons.org/licenses/by-sa/3.0/
- Creative Commons Attribution-Share Alike 2.5 Generic (CC-BY-SA 2.5): http://creativecommons.org/licenses/by-sa/2.5/deed.en
- Creative Commons Attribution-Share Alike 2.0 Generic (CC-BY-SA 2.0): http://creativecommons.org/licenses/by/2.0/deed.en
- Creative Commons Attribution-Share Alike 1.0 Generic (CC-BY-SA 1.0): http://creativecommons.org/licenses/by-sa/1.0/deed.en
- CC0 1.0 Universal (CC0 1.0) Public Domain Dedication (CC0 1.0) http://creativecommons.org/publicdomain/zero/1.0/deed.en
- GNU Free Documentation License (GFDL): http://en.wikipedia.org/wiki/Wikipedia:Text_of_the_GNU_Free_Documentation_License
- License Art Libre (Free Art License): http://artlibre.org

Other Books from Timespinner Press

The Story of a Special Day

Michael Dobson

A series of (eventually) 366 volumes covering everything that happened on your special day! Events, births, deaths, quotes, holidays, and much more. It's like a birthday card they'll never throw away!

US$7.95 print/US$2.99 ebook.

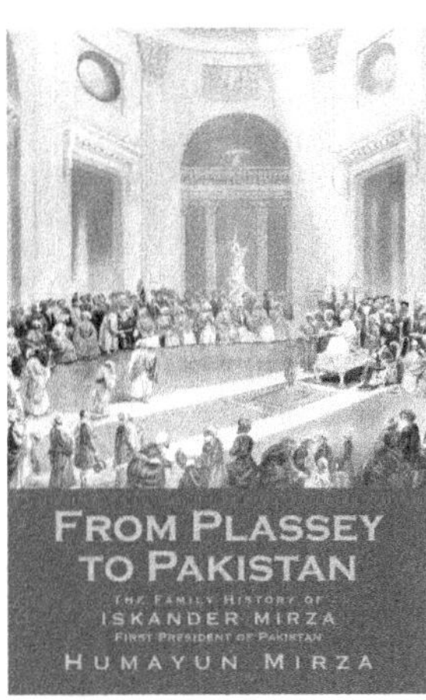

From Plassey to Pakistan

Humayun Mirza

The history of British Colonial India and the formation of Pakistan from the unique perspective of the son of Pakistan's first president and last of the royal line of Bengal, Bihar, and Orissa! This unique historical document tells the inside story of this distinguished family, including the detailed story of the coup that toppled his father from power!

US$27.95 print

A Whole New Navy: America's War in the Pacific

Miles Durr

The most comprehensive and detailed description of America's naval war in the Pacific ever—every battle, every ship, every task force and every task group from Pearl Harbor through the Japanese surrender! A must-have for the collection of every World War II buff!

US$29.95 print

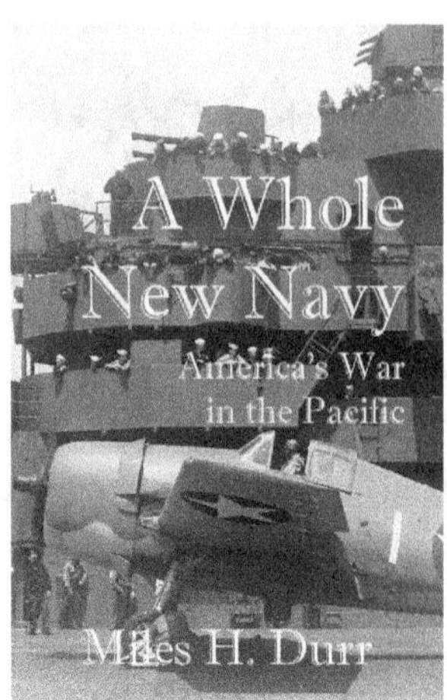

Improbable History: The Weird, the Obscure, and the Strangely Important

edited by Michael Dobson

From the birth of Western civilization to the rescue of Apollo 13, from the Leaning Tower of Pisa to Florence's Duomo, history has often turned on small, improbable details. Whatever happened to the ancient Samaritan people? Why did a fortuitous rainstorm allow the British to conquer India? How did an air raid in Italy lead to the development of chemotherapy? What happened when Albert Einstein met Adolf Hitler on the streets of Berlin? How did the Japanese manage to attack the US mainland using balloons? A cast of award-winning writers tackle some of the strangest tales in history!

US$19.95 print

The Letters of William Philip Schwartz 1842-1855

edited by John F. Schwartz

The 19th century soldier and adventurer William Philip Schwartz wrote a series of vivid and detailed letters chronicling his adventures in the Indian Wars, the Mexican-American War, the Gold Rush, and his term as Marine sergeant aboard the USS Constellation. A pioneer in photography, he took *the first known war photographs*. An unforgettable first-hand look into life in the 19th century!

US$17.95 print

Timespinner
Press

www.timespinnerpress.com